SECRETS X:
Going Your Way

by
Dr. Bob Woodard

SECRETS X:
Going Your Way

by
Dr. Bob Woodard

ISBN 9798880396160

WHY READ THIS BOOK?

It will inspire you to:

1. Appreciate your life
2. Be easily amused and laugh more
3. See change as an opportunity
4. Deal with the unexpected with less fear
5. Experience and use your strengths
6. Realize new demands bring new skills
7. Let yourself receive needed help
8. Listen to the *still small voice* within you
9. Open to new possibilities
10. Share the humorous things in your life
11. Cry more easily with compassion
12. Let go of fixed ideas of who you are
13. Be curious and filled with wonder
14. Open to the inspiration of others
15. Be less concerned about being right
16. Act on a positive impulse just for fun
17. Take a chance; express the love you feel
18. Take a breath and realize no moment is better than this one right now

OTHER BOOKS BY THE AUTHOR
available at:
Amazon.com
Dr. Bob Woodard secrets books

TABLE OF CONTENTS

DEDICATION

To Darla, my wife, my love, my friend and my cheer leader.

I am grateful to all my family members, friends, clients, students, and readers of my books. Your encouragement, love and appreciation have encouraged me to share the lessons, the stories, the insights, and the life lessons we share together.

INTRODUCTION

I've always been curious about the people who enter my life. I wonder what their interests, activities, loves, and goals are and what brings them purpose, meaning, and happiness and, even, what gets in the way of their happiness? It's probably what led me to become a psychotherapist.

In this tenth book of the series, I continue to share my insights and quirky observations and stories about the way many of us secretly think about the world.

You will find a 100 experiences shared in one or two pages. They are designed for easy reading and are meant to be uplifting, insightful and helpful in some way. You will find humor and, surprise endings that will entertain you for hours. The pages can be read over and over.

You will find yourself in these pages. My hope is, as grow and change, these stories and musings will take on new, sometimes deeper meaning. Enjoy yourself!

1. GOING YOUR WAY

We tend to think we plan our lives
Choosing and finding our own way
And selecting the roads we will take
To get where we want to be in the future

But we are more like hitchhikers
We take a chance on finding the drivers
That will take us to our destinations

We tend to catch rides with
A variety of others
We barley know at first
But may choose to travel with
On our life's journey

We make a gesture of interest
So they pick us up
Take us with them
Share the road for a while
Then let us off
Or we jump out
When we think we've gone
As far as we can together

We talk
Share a meal
Make a rest stop
And if we choose

We share a room
A bed
A family
And a life
As we travel through time
On roads we never thought
We'd take
To places we never thought
We would find ourselves

Most of us take our many trips
With ten or maybe twenty people
And travel
Sometimes as drivers
And sometimes being passengers
As we explore together
What lies before us
And then look back at what lies behind

Our lives are less a plan
Than an unchartered adventure
With those whom we choose
To hitch a ride

These are the ones
Who help us select
The roads we take
And how we get there

2. MAKING TIME

Getting together

When
Now and then
Now and again
When we can
Just say when

Not sure we can
Later then

Surely
By appointment
Scheduled
Daily
Weekly
Monthly
Yearly
For the holidays

Can't wait
Let's set a date
For breakfast
Lunch
Or dinner

So
Let's get together
Call me sometime

Or maybe
I'll call you

Sometime

3. THE GIFT OF CLARITY

Most of us remember
Someone
A friend
A family member
A stranger
Who shared just the right words
At just the right time
As you were about to make
A crucial life decision

You were uncertain
About a relationship
A job
A move
An educational choice
Or a matter of health

As you opened to help
Help came
Spontaneously
Someone gently listened
Shared some wise words
Or a simple story
That brought you a new clarity
A sense of certainty
And an answer
You've never regretted

4. DAILY CREATION

As I lay there that morning
Slightly awake
I wondered

How will I choose to spend this day

Will it be with laughter and gladness
Or sorrow and sadness

Will it be with openness and light
Or the darkness of the night

Will it be fun and trouble free
Or troublesome disharmony

Will it be with ease and pleasure
Or resistance
Feeling pressure

Today
Like every day
I can willingly agree
To create
Whatever I foresee

5. OLD FRIENDS

The friends
We left behind long ago
Flit through our minds
Unnoticed

Because they were our friends
Our mental pictures
Refresh our memories
Of the good times
We had together

Such treasures
Bring forgotten pleasures
Back to us for moments even now

Maybe it's time
To just send a thank you note or text

Out of time
Out of nowhere
And just because it would be fun

To offer them the gift
Of knowing you still think of them again
Now and then

6. DAY AND NIGHT

There comes the light of day
And the darkness of night
And so it is
For our delight

There's a time to do
And a time to don't
A time to will
And a time to won't

It is not a fight
Between the two
For each will rest
And then renew

Each day arrives
To bring the light
And then retires
Into the night
There comes the light of day
And the darkness of night
And so it is
For our delight

7. REMEMBERING THE GIFTS

The people you love
Gave you a gift
They may not have known
What that gift was

My mother gave me the gift
Of her gentleness and love of laughter

My dad gave me the gift of his
Caring about my welfare
And the welfare of others

My brother gave me the gift of his
Joy of sports and competition
His simple boyish humor
And his desire to try new things
And explore the issues of the day

My dog Charley
Loved to cuddle
And play hide and go seek
And dance and run around
The house to greet those who entered

Each person you love
Gave you a gift
That you may never have
Put into words

8. WHAT CAN I GIVE AWAY

What can I give
Away today
That I would like to receive

It would be things that
Extend my hope
Healing and happiness
Humor and curiosity
Someone who reminds me to listen
To the still small voice
Within me that responds
To my needs

Someone who listens
If I need to talk
To cry
To laugh
Or remember something important

Someone who offers help
In finding answers
To questions
That may be beyond my awareness

A listening mind
A listening heart
A listening friend

9. MUTUALLY POSSESSIVE

Great wisdom often appears
In unanticipated ways

Long ago
Kung Fu
A television character
Once said
Your possessions possess you

As I drove slowly down
A city street
I noticed the many examples
Of the things that owned me

Houses in need of paint
Leafy lawns
Snow covered driveways

Cars
Trucks
Recreation vehicles

Dogs

And mailboxes

Most days
Our possessions

Have needs
We must fulfill
We took possession of them
So they could serve us
But we overlooked
The fact that we must
In turn
Serve them

10. LIGHT DAY OF THE SOUL

We are easily drawn to think back
And share our experience
Of the dark night of the soul
When relationships changed
Loved ones departed
Income decreased
Illness appeared
Leaving us estranged
From ourselves
Not knowing who we are
And what lies ahead

We do think back
But rarely share our experience
Of the light day of the soul
When relationships stay strong
Loved ones are close
Income is dependably sufficient
We are healthy
Feeling guided
Well and directed
Knowing who we are
And optimistic about what lies ahead

Light and darkness
Fluctuate
But we live most of our lives
In the light
We just don't notice it

11. PRETEND SYNESTHESIA

My fear
Seems to be yellow
It sounds high pitched
Feels prickly
Tastes spicy
And smells like rotting garbage

My anger
Is red
It sounds loud like a siren
It feels hot very hot
It tastes bitter
And smells like a skunk

My sadness
Is blue
Sounds like the lowest string on a base
It feels like a heavy sack of dirt
Pressing on my heart
It tastes like bland gravy
And smells like sweat

My happiness
Is bright green
It's the light sound of peaceful music
It feels soft and smooth
It tastes like delicious whipped cream
And smells like a fresh flower

12. FADE-A-WAYS

Ticking clocks
Blackboards
Ink wells
Fountain pens
Written letters
Typewriters
Newspapers
Landline phones
Memorizing information
Walking to school
Playing outdoors
Dropping in on people
Windows that open
Cloth diapers
Paying in cash

13. WHAT I REALLY WANTED

I was so aggravated at the problem
I thought I wanted
Her to share my overwhelming anger
At the problem
So she could join me
And help justify my tantrum

But a little while ago
I discovered
What I really wanted
When I'm mad at a problem
Was sympathy
Not someone to justify my anger

So I asked for it directly
And she gave me some sympathy
With a hug
To sooth my upset
Rather than joining me
In my aggravation
At a problem
That as usual would soon
Somehow be solved
The next day

14. SORRY DAY

At dinner that evening
On a whimsy
Carolyn suggested
We have a national holiday
One day a year to say we are sorry
For everything we wish we hadn't done
Or said to ourselves or someone else

She suggested we take a day
Every year to say
"I'm sorry"
And get it over with
And out of our system

It would be good for us
And good for the economy

"I'm Sorry"
"I'm Really Sorry"
Phrases we could merchandize
On cards
Tee shirts
Sweatshirts
Hats
Books
Nicknacks

We could create special holiday cruises

And specialty foods and meals
For the occasion

We could take a day off from work
Speeches could be made

We could gather
And wallow
In a day of guilt
Together

In one day each year
We could all reconcile
With God
Self
And everyone we ever met

What a great idea

15. GIVING YOUR PRESENCE

It was a message
Arriving in an instance
Out of the silence
Within him

As he listened
He heard the words
Put simply

He was to share
The presence
The quiet knowing presence
That lies within him

It was to be given to others
Released when needed

An invitation
To a mutual opening
A mutual recognition
A revelation of an easily accessible
Special relationship
That lies within us and between us

A presence of love
To be given away
And no longer hidden
In the silence

16. LOVE UNRESTRAINED

What if we allowed
Food and water
Safety and shelter
Education and the arts
Health and wealth
And freedom

To flow freely
Over the borders
Boundaries
And limitations
Posed by the states
The nations
Ideologies
Identities
Religions
Races
And fixed ideas

What if
We were willing
To share and allow the inspired
Unlimited answers
To become the example
Rather than the exception
In a world of such promise
Possibility
And Plenty

17. TAKING A STAND

Let your children
Stand up
With you
And then slowly
To you
As they stand up for themselves

Stand aside
And let them over-stand themselves
For a while

Don't stand in their way
As they learn to understand
Themselves
And then you

Eventually
All misunderstanding
Will become a new understanding

When they
Have had children
Who will take a stand
As they grow up

18. HAPPY PEOPLE

Open to and remember the people
In your life
Who have decided to be happy

Slowly
Let their faces come to mind
See the smile they brought you
The joy of their company
The little pleasures they shared
As you notice your own smile return

Recall a moment in time
You shared
A meal
A drink
An adventure
A gathering with friends
An amusing secret

Re-bless yourself
With their presence
Now
In some way
Anyway
Keep it simple

19. TWO TIMING

You know you're only supposed
To have one love at a time

Take Maggie
For instance
She was the one
My one and only love

At least for a year

Then I met Annie
She was entrancing
But she let me know
That first night I met her
She didn't have a place to live
At that point

So without telling
Or asking Maggie
I did a crazy thing
I brought Annie home

I thought there would be trouble
Big trouble
But somehow
To my great surprise
They both seemed okay
With this new arrangement

At least until bedtime when
Both of them expected to sleep with me

I didn't know what to do
So finally
I just went to bed

Maggie of course
Just followed me and got into bed
Like she always had

But to my surprise
Shortly after
Annie came into the room uninvited
And got into bed too

What was I going to do

And even more important
What were they going to do
To each other

Well
They both snuggled in close to me

In the morning
They even shared the same breakfast
And doggie water bowl

And that was the way we lived
From then on

20. HEALING HAPPENS

We frequently tell our story
In a loud voice
When we are in physical
Or emotional pain
About what happened
And how we need help and a healing

We let those close to us
Or even strangers
Know
We are hurting and in need

And most of the time
A healing happens
In a relatively short
Or sometimes longer time

But the healing part of the experience
When completed
Is rarely shared
Celebrated
Or dwelled upon
For more than a moment

No one gets sympathy
For a healing

The healing part of the story

Is barely mentioned

We point to our physical
And emotional scars
And tell the story
Of the misery we went through

Our scars are seen
As evidence of our suffering
Not of our healing

Our healing remains
Hidden from the telling of the tale
Even though
It is the most important
Part of the story

The happy ending
Is after all
The point of the story

21. RELATIONSHIPS GO ON

Death ends a life
But not a relationship
These are the words spoken
As the movie
I Never Sang for My Father
Begins

When we have to say goodbye
To a loved one
We miss their physical presence

We long to see them
To touch them
To hear the sound of their voice

They seem to disappear
But
In fact
They leave within us
The essence of their presence

If we are willing
We can experience
An ongoing spiritual presence
That enables us to find peace
Knowing the unfinished relationship
Continues
In a different form

Although they are less visible
We can see the images within
They have left behind
As we continue to talk and share with
them

The love we can experience
Can be extended and healed
In the mystery
Of the afterlife relationship

Our ongoing relationship
Allows us to transcend
All imaginary barriers from the past
To join in an ongoing love
Healing
And closeness
We continue to seek and share

22. MEASURING TIME

In the beginning
There was only
Light and then darkness
Night and then day

As time has passed
We have divided Infinity into
Light years
Millenniums
Centuries
Decades
Years
Months
Weeks
Days
Hours
Minutes
Seconds
And
Nanoseconds

23. PLAYING WITH TIME

You can

Plan it
Watch it
Stretch it
Shrink it
Take it
Make it
Have it
Keep it
Lose it
Put it off
Ignore it
Value it
Waste it
Spend it
Spare it
Share it
Use it wisely
Use it poorly
Remember it
Forget it
Be on time
Or
Run out of it
Now
Then
Or in the future

24. OUR HAUNTING AGENDAS

Later in life
I became aware
Of how blessed I had been
By a mother who had
No agenda for me
Beyond my being
A kind person
Who enjoyed
Playing
Laughing
And singing

As a therapist
I spent many years
Helping people heal
From parental agendas
And expectations
They did not
Could not
Or wanted not
To meet

Let there be no mistake
My mother's lack of an agenda for me
Was not out of neglect
But was an unusually kind
And loving acceptance
Rarely given to many children

Parents often have unique
Often unconscious
But demanding agendas
For their children to carry out

These unmet agendas
Become a life-long source
Of disappointment
For both the generations

After all
What we want to achieve
Who we think we are
Who we want to be
And how we spend our time
Varies between the generations

Sometimes it takes a lifetime
To discover and sort out
What we want and who we are
And who we are in spirit

Life is easier
When it's uncomplicated
Or haunted
By a parent's agenda

A parent who may not
Have carried out
Or far exceeded his own parent's agenda

25. DOIN' TIME

I woke up
Doing yesterday
I guess I wasn't quite finished with it
So I stayed in bed
Until I could let yesterday go

I got out of bed

As I shaved
I started planning the rest of the day
Or at least some of it

I don't recall being present
Right in the moment
You know
Feeling the water on my face
The soap in my hair
The feel of the soft towel
On my face and hands
I don't even recall looking into
My own eyes and greeting myself
In the mirror

I missed that experience
As I bounced around
The time zones of yesterday
And what I was planning
For the rest of this day

In a mind fog
Filled with plans and worries
About what was
Or might be

But once again
I caught myself
In these cluttering- my-mind habits
Losing out
On the precious sensuous moments
Of right now
And the pleasure
Of just plain sharing with myself
The consciousness
Of my right-now experience

26. IT'S TIME TO SPEAK UP

It was only much later in life
Almost at the end
He discovered
That he had made a child's decision
To speak very softly
A display of respect

Or
Looking back
More likely
An unconscious fear
Of angering his dad
If he were loud enough to be
Talking back at him
So to speak

He was very shy
Around adults
Feeling he was to be seen
And not heard
To be a quiet observer
Invisible
Hiding in plain sight

He learned
Not to be curious
About these adults
Creatures from another world

Secret world
Where questions
Personal questions
Were unwelcomed

He was quite content
Safe in the world
Of his childhood
Where he was expected to play
And entertain himself
And learn the skills of youth
With his friends

Speaking up
Seemed always to be inappropriate
And dangerous
In the world of the aliens
The adults

It took him a long time
To see himself as an adult
An alien
Allowed
To speak aloud
In a full-throated voice
To be curious about
And question others

When does one
Where does one
And how does one

Get permission
From himself
To be an adult
When the unwarranted
Fears of childhood
Lie so deeply hidden
In the layers of our own
Unconscious
Bull Shit

27. NO MORE SURPRISES

He thought he was alone

In exasperation he blurted out loud
I don't want any surprises today
Or any day
I want things to go the way
I expect them to go

I want things to stay the way I like them

Is that too much to ask

I don't want my relationships to change
Any unexpected changes in my health
I don't want things to get more expensive
Or any new demands for my attention

Is that too much to ask

I don't want any surprises
I want to know ahead of time
What's going to happen

Is that too much to ask

Then he heard a voice from a stranger
In a nearby stall say
Yes, that's too much to ask

28. AN EASIER WAY

You get to do something
Verses
Having to do something

You let yourself sleep
Verses
Trying to sleep

You let someone help you
Verses
Getting someone to help you

You get it right sooner or later
Verses
Getting it right the first time

You do something
Verses
Trying to do something

29. LOVING OUT LOUD

I don't recall
When
Nor why
The phrase came to mind
But I heard it
Clearly

Love out loud

These words followed me
As I wandered through the day
Wondering what this message
Might release into the world

So I simply started to share
My gratitude
And love out loud
Spontaneously
To those
Who crossed my path
That day

With ease
Not embarrassment
I blurted out
My appreciation
For each person's smile
Thoughtful act

Sense of humor
Special word of encouragement

30. WHISPERS

Secrets softly spoken
Confessions shared

Gossip
Fears
Words that often bring tears
Things you dare not do
But dared someone else to

Playful pranks
Warnings unheeded

Answers needed
When cheating succeeded

Whispers in the day
Whispers in the night
Some about what's wrong
Some about what's right

Sharing secrets

Whispers delight

31. NOT JUST AN ANIMAL

He said our basic animal nature
Is to defend our sources
Of food sex and territory

It was a startling observation
It struck me as simple
Profound
And true

Though I didn't like the implications

It seemed to limit
Us to an animal nature
That ignored our spiritual nature

The great advances of
Humanity
Lie in our dreams and efforts
To share our food
To spiritualize our relationships
And to share our land
And possessions with others

It is the rising above
Our animal nature
That has led us to find and express
The gift of our often hidden
God-like nature

32. THE SEVEN DWARFS

Have you ever noticed that five
Of the seven dwarfs
Were named for their medical
Or emotional problems

Grumpy
Dopey
Bashful
Sleepy
And Sneezy

Doc must have treated them all

But he only had success
With one of his five little patients
Happy

I wonder what Happy's name was
Before he was successfully treated

33. PAST LIVES

We not only think
We can visit the past
We think we can change it

We believe that the past
Is immortal
Cannot die
Disappear
Or be gone forever

It haunts us

We keep returning to the past
To change it
Because we think we can't carry on
With the way it was

Why else would
We visit an unhappy time
We think is a place
We can visit

We do like to visit the past
But we wouldn't want to live there

Maybe
We don't even have to visit it that often

34. UNENDING DREAMS

I always thought
I would see you again

But somehow
I knew
You would fade
Into my past life

After all
The way we ended
Seemed clear at the time
It wasn't working for both of us
Or perhaps
One of us

Yet now
So many years later
It's not as clear what was missing
Or perhaps present
Between us

We didn't talk about it
At the time we parted
Too painful I guess

At first
We would suddenly
But briefly
Break up

Then return to each other on and off
With no final goodbyes
In mind

But we drifted apart
And the distance
In time and places grew
As new people led us
Into another life

But we always keep
Our unrealized dreams
With us
Wondering
If we would ever meet again
In the years to come
To learn how
Our unending dream
Or potential nightmare
Might have turned out

35. DREAM TAPPING

He said
To his trusted friend Creig
I heard these words
This morning
Spoken clearly to me from within

Tap into your dreams
And abandon your nightmares

It was a well-crafted message
Reminding me
That I need not finish
Nor explore my nightmares
No matter how entertaining
Or seductive their misery
Hopelessness and fury might be

Clearly
Nightmares do not come
To bring happiness
Hopefulness or peace of mind

It is our dreams not out nightmares
That tap into the
Source
Of our positive life changing experiences
And lead us to the life
We find enjoyable and worth living

36. LETTING GRACE HAPPEN

I don't know how it happened
She said
But I let go of my need to control
To know what was going to happen next
To understand beforehand how
Plans
Relationships
Even the days weather
Was going to turn out

Instead I began living
In this very present moment
Free of worry about things
I could not
And now would not
Try to control ahead of time

I started to let things happen by grace

It was with an awareness
Of a presence
A spiritual presence
That would guide me
When I would open
And *let* things happen

It was a knowing without worry
Or the need to be in charge

Of People
Places
Or things

Living
Loving
And simply being alive
Became easier
And less complicated

I found myself trusting
In a new kind of relationship
With an unfolding life
Full of the surprising gifts
Of grace in the present moment
Of each day

37. ELEVATED

Elevation seems to be our goal
We want to move up in the world

How do we get from the lower levels
To the higher levels in life

We take steps to elevate ourselves
So we can move to the top

But there is another way
In 1853
We found an easier way
To elevate ourselves

The elevator was invented

In the overcrowded cities
We began to build
Taller and taller buildings
To house people

At first the rich lived on the lower levels
While the poor had to climb many stairs
To rise to reach their levels of living

The elevator changed the way
We moved up to be classy
The rich could now live higher

To overlook others
And beyond the poor
Who were living beneath them

Over time
Technology
Seems to have elevated us
To living higher
And faster
Even if we're poor

38. A NATIONAL SAVIOR

What is this urge we have
To surrender our freedom and well-being
To a Ruler
A Royalty
A Beneficent Leader
A Holy Man
Who would take care of us
Make things simple
Determine the truth for everyone
Tell us what we need and deserve
One who would determine who to love
And who to hate
Who is important and who is not
Who is to be well-off and who is to be
poor
Who is to be educated
And who is to be ignored

Our American forefathers wisely resisted
This urge to have a God-like person
Return to the Thrown
Hoping he would save us
From having to cooperate with
Care about and love each other
Enough
To save each other from tyranny

39. THE UNEXPECTED

Yesterday
He unexpectedly
Discovered that he expected everything
To be expected

He was upset
When the unexpected
Occurred anyway

But as he looked back on his life
He could see that much of the
Unexpected
Could be expected

And that much of the expected
Unexpectedly did not happen

On the other hand
He was often surprised that the
Expected did happen

Today
He made the unexpected
One of his expectations

He was unexpectedly relieved
And unexpectedly happier

40. KNOW THY SELVES

She said to her friend
You're a therapist
What is therapy anyway

He said
It's about getting to know yourselves
Yes
I mean selves

First you learn to notice
You talk to yourself all the time

As you begin to listen to yourself
You become aware
One of you is talking
And the other is listening

You begin to hear what
Each self is saying
And discover the difference
Between them

Then you're encouraged
To notice the feelings each part of you
Creates

One tries to make you happy
The other to make you unhappy

You've sought therapy
Because you're fearful
Angry or sad

She said
So that's why therapists keep asking you
How you feel

Yes
Knowing what you are feeling
Allows you to connect to the inner source
Your unhappy self

Soon you begin to learn to choose
Which inner source to listen to
The observing wise
Compassionate and helpful voice
Instead of the overly judgmental
Immature
And misery-making self

It may take a long time
Perhaps a lifetime
But in the end
You can learn how to talk to yourself
In a loving and caring way
That makes you
Enjoy being with yourself

41. ANGER'S NOT BORING

Anger comes to protect me
When I need to defend myself
From threats and danger

It arrives at the speed of thought
With a surprising jolt to my senses

It's intense
To sense the power of anger
Coursing through my veins

It jumps to my defense
Even when there is no real danger

It offers me surprise protection
From the danger of being bored to death

Anger gets lonely
And restless in quietness
And routine
So it brings excitement
And entertainment
In the quiet moments
When nothing seems to be happening

It pulls us back into old miseries
To refight old battles
Past arguments

And regrets
It arrives in nightmares
Daymares
And future fears

If it fails to make my past life
Or imaginary future life exciting enough
It leads me to turn on
The stream of imaginary dangers
That fill the airways

Anger entertainers us
Unencumbered by reality
As it interrupts
The peaceful
Safe
And pleasant moments
We forget to enjoy

Anger's not so much my friend
Who defends me against danger
As it is my entertainer
That defends me against boredom

42. SCARING OFF THE HELP

I used to think my anger
Would give me control
Over something
That was clearly
Beyond my control
Knowledge
Skill
Or current capability

There seems to be a part of me
And maybe you
That thinks
Yelling at a problem
Will fix it

Only later in life
Was I to discover
Although embarrassed to admit
My anger was a cry for help

I know it was a cry
Not just a demand for help
'Cause I would not become dangerous
But loud and unruly

The anger of others
Did not seem like a cry for help either
They just seemed to be mad

Sometimes I thought it was
At me
And that made me angry
In return

Now it's clearer
My anger
And the anger of others
Is a disguised
And misguided
Way to seek help
Without admitting it

After all
It doesn't really make sense
For me to frighten off
The source of help
And the helper I need

But the truth is
Despite my discovered wisdom
I sometimes treat myself
To a tantrum
And yell at a problem
'Cause I'm too lazy
And embarrassed
To ask for help

43. ANGER JUST IN TIME

Anger
Is a jumpy time-traveler
It leaps between time zones
Present past and future

Anger may pop into the present moment
To fend off a real threat
Like a physical or verbal assault

But anger prefers to come to life
By reliving imaginary threats
From the past

It's right at home
In our creative nightmares
And daymares

It lives in our own
Or shared imagination
About the old and scary future
We continue to imagine

44. LOVE REMEMBERED

Their beloved daughter
Was now
In hospice care

The family
Remained close knowing
Caring and reassuring her
That love and life itself goes on
In mysterious ways

In an inspired moment
Her mother and sister
Decided to have her name
Tattooed on one of their wrists
Where it would be visible
A way to reassure her
That she would be
Lovingly and actively remembered
Each day of their lives

She wept when they revealed
Her name would be there
On her mom's and sister's wrists

A loving reassurance
To her that their precious love
Would be with her each day

45. MOUNTAINS

Sometimes
We make mountains
Out of mole hills
Creating imaginary
Challenges
That we can simply step over

Sometimes
We make mountains
Out of mountains
Challenges
We need to face
And prepare for
As we gather a party
Of fellow climbers
Experienced experts
And resources for the climb

Sometimes we don't know
The difference
Between a mountain and a molehill
Until we calm down
And look up

46. HEALING WORDS

In our moments of darkness
And doubt
What do we need
When we pray
Unsure and unclear
At the deepest level of our being
What is it we are seeking

When we are adrift
In our sea of overwhelming worries
When we feel alone
Disconnected
However momentary
From ourselves
Our purpose
And our meaning
What is it we long for

We need to hear
These simple words of reassurance
From those we love

You matter
You matter to me

These are the missing words
With a healing power
We need

47. THE LONGEST RACE

THE RACE AROUND THE SUN!

| MERCURY | 88 Days |
| VENUS | 225 Days |

EARTH	1 Year
MARS	2 Years
JUPITER	13 Years
SATURN	29 Years
URANUS	84 Years
NEPTUNE	165 Years
PLUTO	249 Years

MERCURY WINS

48. A NEW FRIEND

We tend to think of old friends
From yester-year
As if having new friends
Were only part of the past

I discovered
There's no age limit
To having a new friend

Unconsciously
I must have thought it was too late
In my life
To have one of life's great delights
Having a new friend

New friends mix with you
And blend with you
Making you feel their presence
And your own
Hinting
And then confirming
That you both matter

Friends restore the warmth
And fun and pleasure
Of a shared life

49. IN PRAISE OF SILLINESS

It seems that silliness
Is reserved for very young boys
And a few little girls

Soon they are told not to be so silly
So they will take you seriously

We outlaw silliness so it will not spread
Beyond childhood

Yet silliness
It's so much fun
It brings us to irrepressible laughter
Smiles and the freedom
Not to make sense
As we make silly faces at each other

For adults
There's one exception to the silliness rule
If we slosh enough alcohol down
Silliness is allowed to show up
And loosen us up
To relax
Dance and sing
In our own silly way

And it's okay

50. HIDDEN SHADOWS

The dark shadows within us
Stay hidden
Until they are revealed
By the inner light

Dark shadows are the negative intentions
We hide from ourselves
By seeing them only in others

We think nastiness and hostility
Is out there and not within us
Noticing our own shadows
Allows us to be humble and forgiving

Within also
Are golden shadows
These shadows are the loving gifts
Of grace, caring and generosity
Talents and the creativity
We hide from ourselves
Qualities we find mostly in others

We think great love and abilities
Are only out there and not within us
Until we let our inner light
Shine on the precious gifts
We've been hiding
In our golden shadows

51. FAMOUS PEOPLE

Do you know any famous people
What I really mean is
Do any famous people know you
And know your name

Chances are you don't know any
Or perhaps you know one or two
How come you don't have a relationship
With a famous person

When I asked myself this question
I only knew one temporarily
Famous person

I don't remember
Avoiding famous people
But I also don't remember
Trying to purposefully
Seeking them out

I suppose
If you knew five famous people
Who also knew you
You might be a famous person

It's just one of my odd questions
That led me to ponder aimlessly

52. JUST AN OBSERVATION

Many
Perhaps most people
Like to explore the outer world
Columbus is one among many
Who has navigated
Discovered and felt driven
To see and experience
What's out there
And gather to tell us about it

Inner world people also
Like to get together and share
Their experiences and discoveries

What has often gone undiscovered
Is that outer world people
And inner world people
Tend to find each other boring

53. TREE BREEZES

As I looked out my window
The branches of the stately trees
Filled with the lush leaves
Of summer
Stood still
Motionless
Quiet
Waiting for the breeze
An anticipated arrival
That would bring them together
In motion
And a swaying
As if music were playing
While they danced in the wind

Trees and the wind
The visible and invisible
Have a special relationship

In each other's absence
There is a longing
A yearning
As they wait
To touch
And hold and move together
As they come to life
No longer alone
They join in the oneness of motion

54. PUZZLED

She said
How could I be wrong when I have such
Sorrowful tales about how he left me?

How could I be wrong when I have such
Anger about how he done me wrong?

How could I be wrong when I sacrificed
Everything to help and please him?

How could I be wrong when I started
Drinking to kill the pain of my
Disappointment in him?

How could I be wrong when I was right
To hate and despise him
And let him know it?

How could I be wrong to quit my job
And start going out with others guys
Because he was ignoring me?

How could I be wrong when I stayed
With Him year after year waiting for him
To change his hurtful ways?

I ask you one more time
How could I be wrong?

55. SPACING OUT

Half of life as we knew it
Has left the building
And is moving into the invisible world
Of digital nowhere

Buildings
Are becoming historical monuments

Education is moving out
Of school buildings

Religion is moving out
Of churches and temples

Money is moving out
Of bank buildings

White collar work is moving out
Of office buildings

Relationships are moving out
Of homes

Buying things is moving out
Of stores

And entertainment is moving out
 Of theatres

Like turtles
We carry our buildings
With us
Wherever we go

56. WHEELING FRICTION

It's the wheels on cars
Planes and trains

It's the wheeling and dealing
In business

As our little minds work
The wheels spin
To make the wheels of industry turn

We discover that without
Wheels and friction
We merely spin our wheels
Unable to move forward

57. HOPE

Hope is not just a word
It's a power
It's a choice
It's faith
It's a way of seeing the possibilities
To come

It's a decision to believe
A way of seeing what is
And beyond
To what can be

It brings patience when it is needed
And strength to create and share
And manifest
What we can imagine

It's the future in the present
A way of being
A way of believing
In the positives
Pleasures
The power of hope

58. TOMORROW

The character said to Denny Crane
Aren't you afraid of tomorrow
Denny replied
I don't live for tomorrow

This got me to wondering

Am I afraid of tomorrow
Hmmm
Sometimes I do fear
What might happen tomorrow

And then I wondered
Could I honestly say
I don't live for tomorrow
Yes
Some part of me does live for tomorrow

As I let this new awareness in
I felt a shift in my intentions
That is
To spend more time on the pleasures
Of this day and less time worrying
About the maybe-problems of tomorrow

Then as if on que
The little voice inside me began to sing
The Sun'll Come Out Tomorrow

59. A QUIETING PRESENCE

I see the love in your eyes
hear the love in your voice
Your love touches my soul
In your presence
I find peace of mind
In your care
I find kindness
And ease

When the winds of trouble arise
I find you here in the eye of the storm
And rest in your presence
Strengthened for what is to come

60. GRATITUDE'S GIFT

Our near-heaven experience
Is a fully realized state of gratitude
Overwhelming gratitude
For our surroundings
For our relationships
For the human angels
That surround us
With the necessities
Food
Water
Clean air
Medical care
Beauty
Opportunities
Entertainment
Meaningful activities
And
Love

When my mind
Body
And soul
Overflows with gratitude
I open myself
To this near-heaven experience

61. TASTEFUL

Have you ever noticed
Somethings you say
Leave a taste
In your mouth

Some are sweet
Tasty
And refreshing

Others
Can be tasteless
Sour
And too bitter

Not everything that comes
Out of your mouth
Is worth sharing

62. PUTTING OUT NIGHT FIRES

In the middle of the night
He had too many thoughts
And they were spreading like wildfire

He wanted to pour water
Onto these worries
And drown them out
So he could sleep

He noticed he was sweating
Took a deep breath
Paused for a moment
And then somehow
He heard the words
Worrying isn't that important

Startled
He replied
Worrying isn't that important???

Yes
It's just old garbage
You set on fire nearly every night
It heats you up and keeps you awake

Do something useful
Piss on your worries
Put them out
And go to sleep

63. PEACE

There is a peace
That surpasses
All
Understanding

It is an experience
Of transcendence

Free of the need to understand
What cannot be understood

It is a release from the limitations
Of the thinking mind
It is a knowing
That is beyond the intellect

It is a resting place
A peace
That only our soul can recognize
And welcome
Into awareness

64. IT'S ALL IN YOUR HEAD

You can use your head
To get ahead
By getting a head start
As you head out the door

You can face the future
Or the facts
Or yourself
In the mirror

You can be a highbrow
Or a lowbrow
And use your furrowed brow
To browbeat someone
Or even yourself

You can see ahead
As you keep your eyes on the prize
Or look someone in the eye
With your bright eyes
Or your evil eye
As you eye someone

You can keep your nose clean
Or to the grindstone
Have a nose for a story
Or just be nosey

You can purse your lips
Be tight lipped
Lippy
Or use your loose lips
To sink ships

You can stick out your tongue
Wag your tongue
Or bit your tongue

You can be rather cheeky

Just don't lose your head
There are so many things
It allows you to do
And it's just in your head

65. SAFELY HOME

Henry's parents died early
Leaving him alone
On his own to seek
A safe place
A shelter
He could call home
A place where he would find protection
From those who might cause him trouble
Or bring him harm

He searched along the beaches
Where he had been left
Alone

As he searched
He discovered others like himself
And noticed they were armored for life
In a hiding place
They carried with them

Like others of his kind
He found himself among friends
Who felt comfortably at home
In the safety
Of their own tortoise shells

66. LOVE UNEXPRESSED

Love unexpressed
Is still
Love

Unexpressed

67. INSPIRATION IN OUR MIDST

When Jim first arrived
He was accompanied by
Some of his relatives
I saw him in the distance
And realized
He had a white cane
He was blind

I wondered if this
Senior Independent Living Community
Was the right place for him
How could he find his way around
Would he need more care and staff help
Than I thought he would find here

A week after he arrived
The community of forty or so
Had already gathered
In the large atrium
For the weekly happy hour
We waited thirty minutes
But were told the scheduled entertainers
Cancelled at the very last minute

What were we to do
For entertainment now

Someone knew Jim played the piano

So he was asked and agreed
To play for us
He was taken over to the seat
At the grand piano
Everyone paused and took a breath

As he performed a ripple of wonder
Flowed through the crowd
As he played familiar tunes for an hour
He wowed us with his musical talent

We knew then and there
His presence was going to be
A great gift to the community

Soon he was helping others
Troubled by their failing sight
Teaching them to use their smart phones
And finding cheaper modes of transport
To appointments, shopping
And entertainment

With humor and obvious intelligence
He amazed us as he participated in most
Of the many activities and groups

When faced with life's challenges
We found Jim to be a loveable
Inspiration who had learned to say
Yes, I can
When so many of us were saying
No, I can't

68. A FLOOD OF TEARS

The voices of hatred and hostility
Adversity and violence
Are overwhelming us

Maybe we should all cry out loud
Cry together
Maybe we should wail as one
In a moment
A day
A week
A year of utter
Tearful sadness

Maybe we should
Fill the world
With the sound of our hurt and pain

Perhaps it's time to hear
The sound of multitudes
Crying in unison
So the voices of hatred
Are drowned out
In a flood of tears
That calls us
Back to the shores of Love
Again

69 A HARD DAY

The hardest part of our day
Is our resistance to it
That resistance
Rubs us the wrong way
Ruffle our feathers
Drags us down
Messes us up
Makes us pout
Furrows our brow
Tires us out
Makes us sigh
Makes us cry
Pains us
Strains us
And drain us

Let's not fight it
Let's delight
In it

And cooperate
With our day

70. IT DEPENDS

Is the chameleon red, green, or brown
It depends

Is H2O, ice, liquid, or steam
It depends

Are the clouds of sunset
White, orange, yellow, red, or pink
It depends

Are people fearful, angry, sad, or happy
It depends

Will you find true love
It depends

Will you make enough money
It depends

Will you like your new job
It depends

Will your next meal be delicious
It depends

Can you be happy without knowing
Already how things will turn out
It depends

71. RELEASE YOUR DAY

Release your grip
On the day
Let it go
Let it slip away
Into the hands of the Unknown
It will point the way

As the day unfolds
Welcome what appears
In each precious moment
Notice again today
The unexpected obstacles
Haven't come to stay
Consider them
A diversion
A distraction at play
You'll find a way
To use them or
Make them go away

They always do

72. BEYOND EXPECTATIONS

When our expectations are exceeded
We call it a miracle
We are happy
And want to celebrate

When our expectations are not met
We call it a problem
We are unhappy
We pout
And complain

When miracles or problems occur
We praise or blame
God
The "world" or circumstances

We never praise
Or blame
Our expectations
Our flawed expectations
For problems or miracles

Behind the scenes
The secret source
Of our unhappiness and happiness
Seems to depend on
Our favored expectations

Maybe we need to go beyond them
Let them slip out of our minds
And out of our lives
And watch what happens
As we let life
Transform
Or Exceed
Our limited and troubling
Unmet expectations

73. LOVE IN TIME

Lately
He seemed to be living
Or was it looking in the past
For the love he felt as a child
In the safe presence
Of his loving parents

Later he was finding himself
Or was it
Losing himself back in time
At the age his parents
Had died
Wanting to go back in time
To be with them
Again

Today
He thought maybe
He should look to the future
To find new location
A new life
And leave the present behind

Then he wondered
Why am I looking
To the future

As the place in time
When he could be happy again

Somehow
He was shifting between the past
And the future
Unable to stay
In the present moment

Where the presence
Of the love he was seeking
Was quietly present
And waiting for his return

74. FAIRY TALES

In the dead of night
The storyteller within you
Loves to take you into your imagination
Of unpleasant scary situations
Where you find yourself
Struggling to escape your fears

You cannot imagine
How to escape
Since you are unaware
You are the victim of your
Own clever storytelling

Your best chance for escape
Is to scare yourself awake

Once awakened
You may catch your breath
And begin to wonder
Why you had such a bad nightmare
Sometimes you return to your sleep
And back into the story you're afraid of
To find out what will happen

It never occurs to you that you
Are the anonymous teller of the tale
In which you became the main character
In your own late-night entertainment

75. THE MISSING PIECES

We went through a time
Of isolation and boredom
Without the people
Places and familiar routines
That used to fill our days

The emptiness
Brought a surge of demand
To return to the past

Some turned to old jigsaw puzzles
To fill the emptiness of their days

People bought new 5oo piece puzzles
Or searched for some old ones
Stored in their closets or basements

In the process
Of putting the puzzles together
They often discovered
Pieces of the puzzle were missing

Puzzled about what to do now
Some became frantic
And began turning their homes
And lives upside down
Trying to find the missing pieces

At least it was something to do

76. A PREDICTABLE ESCAPE

Few of us are comfortable
Living in the unknown

We quickly leave the present moment
And leap into someone's imaginary
future

We flip on our favorite form of media
Seeking the assistance
Of the professional predictors
Who attempt to foretell the future
The weather forecasters
News and talk show hosts
Stock market advisors
Mediums and sooth sayers
And other experts
Who attempt to tell us about the future
Of our relationships
Our health
Our love lives
And our next lives

Of course we could choose our own
Pleasant predictions
About an imagined future
Where everything works out
Eventually
For our good

Or we could simply stay
In the present
Enjoying the sounds
Sights
Smells
Tastes
And feeling of this very moment

We might discover
The present is a resting place
Rather than a dangerous place to be

77. AN UNCHANGEABLE FUTURE

He came into life
Knowing the unchangeable future
That had been predetermined
For him by God

Each and every experience
Every choice
He would make
Would already be known to him

As a condition of his birth
He had agreed
To live what was laid out
Before him
Without deviation

He was never to reveal to anyone
That he knew ahead of time
What was to come
And what was going to happen

He was always to pretend
That he and everyone else
Had choices to make
Options to choose from
And that nothing about the future
Was really known

He was to feign surprise
Intense fear or anger
Or disappointment
When things didn't go the way
Others thought they should go

He knew there was no such thing
As a real surprise
Or that things could be out of order

In time he began to realize
He was beginning to lose interest
In living
He felt like he was dying of boredom

One day in desperation
He decided to tell his secret
That he always knew exactly
What was going to happen next

He finally shared this with his friend
Too his surprise
His friend said she had the same secret

They both did die early
Out of shear boredom

But that too was
Of course
Part of the plan

78. THE SECRET SELF

It was one of those days
They were in the neighborhood
Going door to door
Asking if you wanted to know God
Presumably
The God of their understanding

I decided not to answer the door
But their presence was helpful
It got me to wondering
Not if I wanted to know God
I did know God
But the question became
Did I want God to know me

In a relationship
You want to know someone
But you are not sure you want them
To know you
Until you trust they will accept you

Then you're willing to share more
But
Interestingly
Not all

So my question became
Do I want to share all

With the God of my understanding
I discovered
I wasn't sure I could share all
With myself
Let alone God

So I decided
To share more
With my loving God
And go even deeper
Into our relationship
So together
We could find out
About my
Self

79. GOODBYE PAIN

It's time
To hang on to a relationship no more
That's what pain is for
To tell us once again
It's time to let go
Of someone
Something
Some thought
Some story

We are now to let them go
Like tears that flow
In goodbye pain

Pain doesn't come to stay
But to go away
When it's no longer needed

Why do we resist its loss
Why do we wallow
In our sweet and bitter sorrow
Sharing our stories and songs
Of unhappy memories
Old wounds
And grievances
Thinking they're a gift of some kind

80. DON'T FORGET TO FLUSH

She realized
She was finally emotionally drained
She had flushed away the build up
Of accumulated anger
Fear and sadness
That was clogging
The flow of her happiness

Her growing hatred
Worries and regrets
Had gotten backed up

She needed help
To clear the obstruction
Within her
And remove the wasted
And blocked emotional energy

It was time to let is go
So love could flow
And flush away the debris
Called unforgiveness

81. UNDUET

Many people like to sing
But avoid singing in a duet
Somehow it seems too personal
To sing as a twosome

It's easier to hide
In a trio
Or a choir

There's something
About sharing the senses
Mind free
Making music together
In harmony or unity

Just the two of us
Seems too intimate
To sensual a way to
Make music
Alone together

82 FAKE TIME

John said to her
It's so nice to be with you
In real time again

She smiled and teasingly said
Have you ever been with me in fake time

He sheepishly admitted
I have
But now I won't have to be
With you only in my imaginary past
Or my imaginary future
As often

He probed her
Saying
How about you
Have you secretly
Been with me in fake time

As her face turned red
With embarrassment
She replied
Well John
Maybe it's time
To really do something together

83. PRICKELITIS

It comes in many forms
It's an annoyance

Sometimes it takes form
It has many points
And makes points
That are meant to pierce
Our minds
Our skin
And even our hearts
With annoying persistence

Sometimes it is formless
It's just an upsetting feeling
That gets our attention
And seems to come from nowhere

It increases our fear
Our grumpiness
And our dim view
Of the world and the future
Making it seem
Dark and empty

It's fed by our attention
And makes us cry
Or yell
Or try to run away

They say it's prickelitis
It's a mental illness
That takes over our mood

Some look for a cause
Some will say
It's an allergy
Probably to pickles

But
More likely
It's really a reaction
To prickles

But that makes no sense

84. A PLACE IN TIME

Where will I spend this day
In this place called time

Will I go to the past
What will I find there
Fun
Trouble
Problems
Old friends
Fond memories

Or will I go to the future
What will it be like
What changes will come
To the world
To my world
How will I change it
And how will it change me

And how much time
Will I spend in the present
Just enjoying the consciousness
Of being alive now

I am free
A time-traveller
In the spaces and places
Of time

85. WHAT TO THINK

He wasn't sure what to believe
So he kept looking for his beliefs
In someone else's mind

He would ask someone
What they thought
And then agreed with them

But then someone else
Would say they disagreed
With that someone else
So he agreed with another
Someone else

But then he found himself
Disagreeing with himself

So he tried to get someone else
To agree with him
So he would know what he believed

But they wouldn't agree
To think the same way

So he decided to stop trying to know
What to think
Until everyone agreed with everyone else

He's still waiting for that to happen

86. THE GOODBYE GIFT

We underestimate the value
Of agreeing to say goodbye
At least for now

We tend to resist rather than assist
In our goodbyes

We thought we agreed
To stay close forever

But sooner or later the time may come
To give ourselves
The needed gift of a loving goodbye
And the quiet sharing of tears
Change and parting brings

Sometimes
We must wave goodbye to our past
As we find ourselves waving hello
To our future
Without exactly knowing why

87. LISTENER'S LAMENT

I was noticing
Things about people who talk a lot

As you sit with them
Words spill out of their mouths
Like marbles
Pouring sound
Onto to the table between you
Making noise that never seems to stop

They treat their own silence
As a wasted space
A vacuum of soundless emptiness
Needing to be filled
Quickley and loudly
Before you can sneak a word in edgewise

Talkers try not to pause
Or breathe so they keep their words
Close together
Lest someone jump into an empty space
Between them
And start to speak

Talkers will always say
We had a nice talk
But they would never say
We had a nice listen

88. SEXLESS WORDS

Some words
Have lost their masculinity

Chairman
President
Boss
Actor
Minister
Ambassador
Bread winner
Sargent
Officer
Engineer

Some words have gained
Their masculinity

Single parent
Mr. stay-at-home Mom

Some words remain the same
Garbage man
Trash man
Manhole Cover
Bum

Spouse Abuser
Tyrant

And perhaps most confusing
Is a left over
Called the mail woman

89. REBOOTING YOUR MIND

He watched
As he typed the words
That flowed from his mind
Through his fingers
Onto the screen in front of him

He was pleased
As he paused a moment
Thankful for
This wondrous invention
That served him so well
Enabling him to move his thoughts
From his mind to a page
Allowing him to share his thoughts
With others so easily

He paused again for a moment
And moved his cursor
To the tool bar
At the top of the page
To make an adjustment
And clicked the mouse

To his surprise
The bar of tools
That allowed him
To make all adjustments
Disappeared completely
From the screen

Startled
He began to move the cursor
Around the screen
Attempting to find
The tools he would need
To proceed

Nothing seemed to work
He became frantic
Trying over and over
To restore his power
Over his ribbon of icons
The tools that enabled him
To easily share his words
On the printed page

He felt helpless
And at the super speed of thought
He began to fill his mind
With paralyzing fear
Fear that he would never be able
To get his beloved computer
To ever work again

As he tried over and over
To gain control over the screen
His fear turned to anger
As his anger grew
His ability to think
Continued to shrink

He began to scream
The foul language of frustration
At the screen
As if he could scare his computer
Into working again

He had lost everything he had written
Over the last three days and nights

He was freaking out and he knew it

So he left the room
Poured a cup of coffee
Began to breathe again
And let himself become calm

Then it occurred to him
He might have to try
The ultimate risky solution
One that might obliterate
All of his precious creations
They could die
With a stroke or two
On the keyboard

In a final act of desperation
He did it
He rebooted the computer

Surprisingly
It worked

And the tools of salvation
Reappeared on his screen

He was saved
His work was saved
And another episode of craziness
Was over

90. NIGHTMARES AGAIN

He awoke at three o'clock
In the morning
In the middle of a nightmare

When he got out of bed
He walked quickly to the bathroom
Troubled
Trying to recall
What he had been dreaming about

Great significance has been attributed
To the meaning of nightmares
Over the centuries
The prophets
The psychoanalysts
And the storytellers
Have found them to be profound sources
Of hidden wisdom
So he was trying to settle himself
So he could remember
The content of his dream

And then it happened
He had a profound realization
The real gift of his repeated nightmares
Was to awaken him
So he would not wet the bed

91. INFINITY

Concepts
Allow us to name and classify things
So we think they exist

We have lots of concepts like
A tree
A house
A car
A dog
A person

We often mistake a concept
Or an idea
For an experience
Of something that is changing
And evolving

Astronomers like the concept of infinity
But how can we conceive of something
That has no beginning and no end
Something that expands beyond
The limits of our understanding

Psychologists seem to like
The idea of a self
Self concept
Self esteem
Self worth

Self abuse
Self realization

They seem to think
It's useful
To conceive of the
Self
As a thing

My hunch is that the self
Is an experience
Everchanging and expanding
Without beginning and without end
A God-like experience
Of infinity

92. QUESTIONS

When we don't know what to do
We search for answers
When answer seem beyond our reach
We become frantic

We may be facing a deadline
An encounter
A decision

At such panic points
We forget
To pause
Breathe
And remember
Sometimes good answers
Are not ready
Until we find
Good questions

Pray for the right questions
And then listen

Can I see this differently
Can I get some help
Can I get more resources
Can I get more time
Eventually will I be okay either way

The answers will come

93. A GUILTY MALPRACTICE

As he stood at the pulpit that morning
To the surprise of the congregation
The priest sprayed cold holy water
On the crowd by saying
Guilt is not a spiritual practice

Guilt
He said
Is a way of living in the past
Trying to change
What is over and done

He went on by saying
Spiritual practice is letting go of the past

Let someone
Including yourself know
You are truly sorry
Stop your future offending behavior
And make amends

Chronic guilt
Is emotional self-flagellation
Is feeling bad and sad
About things you cannot change

He went on to say
It may be a holy shock

And confusing to some of you
But God
Is not interested
In your self-punishment called guilt
It separates you from the very love
You are seeking

Guilt is not a substitute
For loving action toward yourself
Or others

As the priest listened to the murmurings
Of shock in the congregation

He suggested
They might want to give up
The non-spiritual practice of guilt
For lent
And take up the spiritual practice of love
Instead

As the hush of silence settled
In the church
He knew it was time
For him to say
Amen

And quickly leave the pulpit
Having shared with them
The startlingly good news
That guilt is not a spiritual practice

94. GROWING UP

Like a seed that is planted
And nurtured
We rise slowly
From the ground of our being
Growing upward
Toward the light

We rise
Outgrowing the expectations
Of what we thought we could be

Fertilized by love
And supportive surroundings
We grow through the seasons
Of life

Nurtured by grace
Attracted to the light
We ascend
Taking an even wider view
And gaining a higher perspective

As we flower
Into what we were meant to be

95. MISCONCEPTION

How do you conceive of your Self
Do you have two ideas of yourself
Opposite concepts

In the discourse between them
Do they create a third idea
Of who you are

Do they have preconceptions
Or pregnant moments
Laboring to give birth
To a perfected self
Only to miscarry and misconceive
And then grieve at the imperfection
Of your creation

Only to start over
With more growing pains
Fleeting self-concepts
Of imagined self-images
Vacillating levels of self-esteem
And self-regard
Trying to self-actualize

Only to realize
You are not a concept
But a relationship
To the Divine
Evolving over time

96. WHITE OUT

He would imagine the scene
Of what he thought was a crime often
Hoping
He wouldn't stay there too long
Imagining
How it all could have gone
Differently
So many years ago

Although his visits were imaginary
He brought the perpetrator
And the past
Back into his life

As he continued to remember
The past and the pain
He wanted to forget
He became the victim
Of his desire to undo
What happened

To help him
Stop using his imagination
To visit the painful past
That blackened his present
His therapist taught him

The white out technique

A healing way
To use his imagination

He was told to take an imaginary
Spray gun of white-out paint
To his next imaginary "visit"
To the crime scene

He was to spray the entire scene
People, faces, objects
The background and surroundings
With a white paint
That covered everything
And made it
Unrecognizably white

If there were words or sounds
Or voices of any kind
The paint would muffle them
Into complete silence

Then and only then
He was to leave
The scene of the crime

A scene he could no longer see
Nor hear
Nor remember

97. GOING BACK FOR A VISIT

There is a sadness about the past
That seems to want
Old times to last
And return to places
And things we've done
With those we've met
And shared our fun

We drift in time to find the past
Reliving times that didn't last
To see ol' friends and have some fun
And finish things we've left undone

Ah
To live again with those we've known
Retelling stories of what we shared
To laugh and kid about our youth
When we broke an arm or lost a tooth

Chances taken mistakes we made
So many experiences we wouldn't trade
Secrets kept and some we shared
Trips we made so unprepared

We met some mates and dated friends
A closeness felt that never ends

The past is not a place we stay
Yet it never goes away

98. A PRESENT

As I enter into this moment
Now
I come into the full consciousness
That I am alive
That I exist

Absorbed in this miracle of being
At one in the overwhelming comfort
And peacefulness
I am experiencing

I let myself slowly grow and expand
As I merge into the unlimited awareness
Of the love
That surrounds and fills me completely

99. FINDING OURSELVES

When we met
We were both leaving relationships
That were falling apart
And we were letting them

When such endings come
We feel lost and on our own
And begin to search
For someone else
Unconsciously hoping
To find our lost selves
With another person

But on the way to the future
Both of us
Were somehow led in another direction
To a spiritual gathering place
To find the part of ourselves
We thought was missing

As we turned inward
We found ourselves
On a spiritual journey

We began to explore
Study
Listen
And openly share

What we were learning
On this inward path
Of searching
We discovered
Within ourselves
And in each other
The loving
Spirit
We had been missing

100. IT WASN'T A PLAN

Some of us planned our lives
But most of us have lived a life
That happened to us

It is not that we didn't have goals
Or aspirations

But our plan was more about
Wanting to try something new
Or escape old circumstances

We may simply have fallen
Into someone else's life
Such as that of a mate
A friend or a relative
Or even a stranger
And decided we'd go with them
And ended up cocreating a new life
In a new place

We didn't so much find the path
But one appeared before us
And we took it

We didn't really plan our lives
We just made a series of choices
That still surprise us
And hopefully please us even now

SOURCES OF INSPIRATION

Darla Woodard, Albert Woodard, Margaret Woodard, Dick Woodard, Todd Woodard, Kim Woodard Jankowiak, Jim Fettgather, Carolyn Gifford, Charley I, Creig Skau, Daniel Maffei, Chuck Sances, Alan Cohen, God, A Course in Miracles, Center for Spiritual Living in Reno, Michael Gott, Mooji, Eckart Tolle

SHARE YOUR REVIEW

Kindle will give you the opportunity to take a few minutes to rate this book and share a few thoughts as a book review. It's a powerful way to encourage others to read and share the books with friends and family. It makes a great gift for the holidays and birthdays. If they enjoy it as you do, they'll be grateful to you, as will I.

All the best,

Dr. Bob

ABOUT THE AUTHOR

DR. BOB WOODARD

Welcome to Dr. Bob's tenth book, *SECRETS X: Going Your Way.* Advanced degrees prepared him to be a psychotherapist, drug and alcohol, and marriage and family counselor. He pursued further studies to become a spiritual teacher and counselor. During his career, he has taught and trained hundreds of clinicians and conducted over 1,000 classes that embrace both spiritual and positive psychology including the teachings of New Thought, *A Course In Miracles* and the Law of Attraction.

He now enjoys being a life coach for solo business professionals and presents workshops on specific ways to leave suffering behind by easing into the daily practice of gratitude, forgiveness, and happiness.

He lives in Reno, Nevada with his gentle, artist wife, Darla. His life is filled having fun and communing with his friends and family. He loves to write and teach, as well as sing and play the ukulele with his band of friends.

OTHER BOOKS BY THE AUTHOR

available at:
Amazon.com
Dr. Bob Woodard secrets books

Made in the USA
Las Vegas, NV
14 December 2024

14211481R00085